Contents

Introduction

to Course & Subjects

Course Outline

This is a four part course designed to help participants learn more about their faith and how to apply it to everyday life, how to study the Bible, explore theology and become more effective leaders.

The subjects and some of the elements covered are:

Bible: Jesus, The Bible & You –

- ★ How to read the Bible devotionally and for study purposes
- ★ Historical background to the Bible
- ★ How to use all the Bible study tools
- ★ How to get revelations from the Bible

Leadership: The Church & Your Leadership Journey – Learn effective leadership qualities and skills that can build your own life and the lives of others, seeing the kingdom of God move forward.

Lifestyle: Following Jesus –

- ★ How to build a strong devotional life
- ★ How to find your purpose in God
- ★ How to live a life that can fulfil your purpose
- ★ How to hear from God

Theology: Faith Foundations – Develop a personal theology in a biblical and thoughtful way that will be a blessing to you and your church community.

Learning Sessions

Once per week for 2½ hours which includes 2 teaching sessions, 1 application session and a 20min break (after session 1).

Teaching Sessions – each week will include 2 x 50 minute sessions in a lecture style.

Application Sessions – each week will consist of 1 x 25 minute group session where homework and previous teaching sessions will be used to stimulate discussion. These sessions will vary in activities including multimedia and role playing etc.

Homework

Each week you will get a small amount of work to complete at home. It should take about 20 minutes to complete and it will be used to stimulate discussion the following week during the group session. There are also some advanced questions for those who wish to do more in-depth study.

Bible Version

Throughout this course the New International Version (NIV) has been used unless otherwise specified.

Many translations can be viewed freely from websites such as: **www.biblegateway.com**, **www.biblestudytools.com** and **www.bible.cc** or on your mobile device using applications such as **YouVersion**. We encourage you to research and find what works best for you.

Before you commence spend a few moments to pray and ask the Holy Spirit to give you eyes to see what the Word is saying to you.

Leadership

The Church & Your Leadership Journey

This subject gives a seven week overview of how to learn effective leadership qualities and skills, which will help to build your life and also help you build into the lives of others.

Recommend Reading

If you want to get a deeper understanding of this subject, below are some recommended resources:

★ Bobbie Houston, **Heaven Is In This House**, (Maximised Leadership, Sydney: 2001)

★ Brian Houston, **For This I Was Born**, (Thomas Nelson, Nashville: 2008)

★ Brian Houston, **The Maximised Life Series**, (Maximised Leadership, Sydney: 2002-2004)

★ John Maxwell, **Developing the Leader Within You**, (Thomas Nelson, Nashville: 1993)

★ John Maxwell, **Developing the Leaders Around You**, (Thomas Nelson, Nashville: 1995)

★ Erwin McManus, **An Unstoppable Force**, (Strand Publishing, Sydney: 2001)

★ Rick Warren, **The Purpose Driven Church**, (Zondervan, Grand Rapids: 1995)

★ Bill Hybels, **The Volunteer Revolution**, (Zondervan, Grand Rapids: 2009)

★ Bill Hybels, **Courageous Leadership**, (Zondervan, Grand Rapids:2009)

Week 1

Introduction

Session 1 – Introduction to Leadership

Leadership is an Example
Your Leadership Journey
Leadership and The Church

Break

Session 2 – A Cause-Driven Church and Life

The Church and It's Cause
The Great Commission
The Cause of Christ and the Vision for the Church
Church Vision and Personal Vision

Session 3 – A Cause-Driven Church and Life

Homework – Personal Vision Statement

Session 1
Introduction to Leadership

Outcomes

By the end of this session, you will be able to:

* Explain what leadership is, in a simple way
* Describe the different levels of leadership, how they're different, and how that constitutes a person's journey as a leader
* Explain how a person's leadership is developed through their involvement in church

Leadership is an Example

Your Leadership Journey

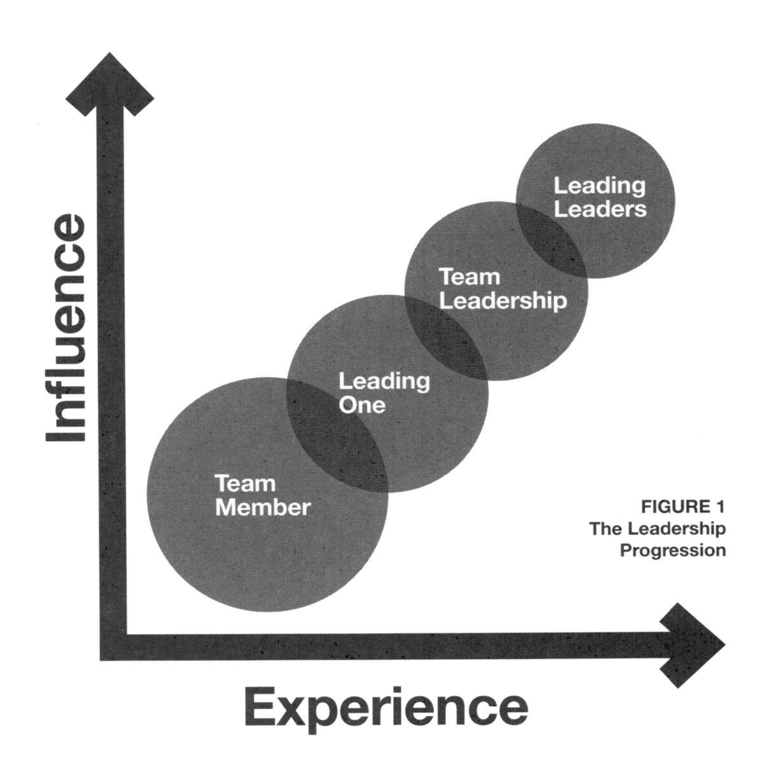

FIGURE 1
The Leadership Progression

Leadership and The Church

Session 2

A Cause-Driven Church and Life

Outcomes

By the end of this session, you will be able to:

* Explain how the Great Commission and the cause of Christ describes the Church's purpose
* Explain the relationship between the cause and a local church's vision
* Explain the relationship between a local church's vision and an individual's personal vision

The Church and Its Cause

The Great Commission

Cause and Vision for the Church

Church Vision and Personal Vision

Session 3
A Cause-Driven Church and Life

A Cause-Driven Church

What reasons might a church have for existing other than the Cause of Christ? (Note this may not be stated, but would still be a powerful factor in that church's culture, e.g., for the comfort of its members.)

Imagine a "cause-driven" church and a "non-cause-driven" church. How do you think they would differ when it comes to the following things:

- ★ Growth
- ★ Evangelism
- ★ Welcoming new people
- ★ Church members involved in serving
- ★ Giving
- ★ Sacrifice
- ★ Change
- ★ Work ethic
- ★ Commitment

A Cause-Driven Person

What are some of the attributes and behaviours you expect to see in someone who is motivated by the cause of Christ? Make a list.

What kind of decisions does a cause-driven person make compared to a non-cause-driven person? Make a list

What sort of things do you do (can you do) to develop the attributes of a cause-driven person?

What sort of things can or do we regularly do to develop the following attributes personally?

Attribute	Behaviours
Vision	
Growth	
Ownership	
Involvement	
Commitment	
Energy	

Homework

Personal Vision Statement

Take some time to write down your personal vision for the following areas. Remember that a good vision statement should be clear and unambiguous, and describe what success in this area looks like. It should also include a list of things which you are currently doing or intending to do to see the vision become a reality.

My leadership in the church

My relationships with other people

My relationship with God

My health

My finances and giving

Week 2

Introduction

Session 1 – What is the Church? (Part 1)
The People of God

Break

Session 2 – A Healthy Church (Part 1)
Gatherings
Atmosphere

Session 3 – What Do The "People of God" Look Like?

Homework – How Did They Do It In The Early Church?

Session 1
What is the Church? (Part 1)

Outcomes

By the end of this session, you will be able to:

* Explain, from scripture, the idea of the Church as the called-out, gathered-together community of God's people
* Explain how this concept is expressed through local churches

The People of God

Session 2
A Healthy Church (Part 1)

Outcomes

By the end of this session, you will be able to:

* Explain, from scripture, how the idea of Church as "the people of God" requires and expresses itself through church gatherings
* Describe and explain some aspects of how their church conducts various forms of church gatherings to fully express "church as community"

Gatherings

Atmosphere

Session 3

What Do the"People of God" Look Like

Discuss the following questions in a small group setting. You may like to write some of your group's answers down.

What are some of the key ingredients that can make a local church a genuine expression of "the people of God"?

List some of the changes we would expect to see in people when they realise and come to experience that the church is God's people. How would they feel?

How should we act as “the people of God” when we gather for our weekend services?

How can you (or do you) help make your local church a genuine expression of “the people of God”? Be very practical.

Homework

How Did They Do it in the Early Church?

Read Acts 2. Focus in on **Acts 2:42-47** which describes how the Early Church related to each other and answer the following questions:

Write down six key words that describe how the people felt about each other.

What practical steps can you find from the Early Church that built the prevailing atmosphere amongst its members?

Are there any ways in which we can relate this to the way we approach "church" today?

What impact did their actions and approach have on those outside the church?

Putting it into Practice

Do these things this weekend in church:
Start a conversation with three people in church this weekend. In a friendly way explore how they feel about coming to church and make a mental note of their responses.

For example you could ask:

- ★ How long have you been coming along to church?
- ★ Do you attend and/or serve in any service in particular?
- ★ What are the main things that attract you to church?

Consider a person on the New People's team at church on the weekend.
How do they make people feel: Welcome, Included, Connected, At home?

Week 3

Introduction

Session 1 – What is the Church? (Part 2))
The House of God

Break

Session 2 – A Healthy Church (Part 2)
Word and Worship

Session 3 – What does the "House of God" Look Like?

Homework – No Barriers in Christ

Session 1

What is the Church?(Part 2)

Outcomes

By the end of this session, you will be able to:

* Explain, from scripture, the idea of the church as the "House of God"
* Trace this idea through the Bible
* Explain how this concept is expressed through local church life

The House of God

Session 2

A Healthy Church (Part 2)

Outcomes

By the end of this session, you will be able to:

* Explain, from scripture, how the idea of church as "the House of God" translates into corporate worship and the ministry of the Word in local church gatherings
* Describe and explain some aspects of how Hillsong does corporate worship and preaching to express "church as the House of God"

Worship & Word

Session 3

What Does the "House of God" Look Like?

Discuss the following questions in a small group setting. You may like to write some of your group's answers down. ***(Note: This exercise focuses on "the House of God". You should get very different answers to the exercises when you focused on "the People of God".)***

What sort of things would you expect to see happening in a local church that was genuinely being "the House of God"?

What should people experience when they are in “God’s House” that they can’t experience anywhere else?

What sort of changes would we expect to see in people when they experience church as “the House of God”?

How can you help make church a genuine expression of "the House of God"?

What ways do you think you can grow so that you can help make church "the House of God"?

Homework
No Barriers in Christ

Read **Colossians 3:8-17** and answer the following questions. You may need to consult other resources:

In verse 11, Paul talks about there being "no distinction in the body of Christ, but rather that Christ is all and in all." How might the following distinctions have manifested themselves in a church or small group context in Colossae?

Distinction between	What is the distinction about?	How might this appear?
Jews and Greeks		
Circumcised and Uncircumcised		

Table continued on the next page...

Barbarian and Scythian		
Slaves and freeman		

What might the modern equivalent of these distinctions and instructions be? How can we avoid this?

Personal evaluation

In this passage Paul lists a number of attitudes we should have toward one another, for example compassion, forgiveness etc.

Select three such attitudes from this list on which you can improve and describe how your relationships with others gets better as you do:

* ______________________
* ______________________
* ______________________

What things can you do this week to improve the attitudes you listed above?

Week 4

Introduction

Session 1 – What is the Church? (Part 3)

The Body of Christ
Key Scriptures
Giftedness of All Believers

Break

Session 2 – Your Spiritual Gifts

The Spiritual Gifts
How Do The Spiritual Gifts Work?
Where and How Do You Use Your Spiritual Gifts?

Session 3 – Identifying Your Spiritual Gifts

Homework– The Use of Spiritual Gifts

Session 1

What is the Church (Part 3)

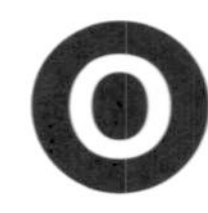

Outcomes

By the end of this session, you will be able to:

* Explain, from scripture, the idea of the Church as the "body of Christ"
* Explain how this concept is expressed through local churches
* Explain the personal implications of the Church a the "body of Christ"

The Body of Christ

Giftedness of All Believers

Session 2
Your Spiritual Gifts

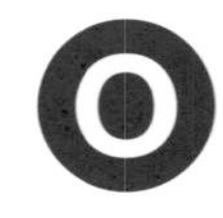

Outcomes

By the end of this session, you will be able to:

* Explain the idea of the priesthood and giftedness of all believers
* Describe the key spiritual gifts
* Explain the origin, identification and development of a person's spiritual gifts
* Explain the pathway in their own local church for people to identify and get involved in using their gifts to serve others

The Spiritual Gifts

How do the Spiritual Gifts Work?

Where and How do You Use Your Spiritual gifts?

Session 3
Identifying Your Spiritual Gifts

"So how do I find out what my gift is?" Often it is best to start by considering what you are passionate about, because you are more likely to develop your gifting in these areas first. Also, where you already experience fruitfulness and acknowledgement from others is also a strong indication of your spiritual gift.

For the purposes of this exercise, we have grouped together the gifts into the following categories:

- Word of wisdom/knowledge/prophecy
- Healing/miracles
- Leadership
- Evangelism
- Teaching
- Service/administration
- Exhortation/giving/mercy

Using the tables on the following pages, to start you thinking about the areas for which you may have a particular gift, place a tick in the box beneath the column which best describes how you feel about the statement. After you have responded to each statement, find the area that contains the most statements with which you strongly agree. If you have responded to each statement as honestly as you can, this will probably represent the area where you are most inclined to be gifted. ***(Note: You do not have to tick a box if you feel that the statement does not apply to you.)***

1 = Strongly Agree **2** = Agree **3** = Disagree **4** = Strongly Disagree

Wisdom/Knowledge/Prophecy

Statement	1	2	3	4
I am comfortable explaining the Word of God to others. I feel God prompts me when I speak.				
I am a fairly good judge of character. I can quickly assess where someone is at.				
For me prayer is a way of life. I find it easy to talk to God whatever I am doing.				
When I give advice to other people it tends to be well received.				

Healing/Miracles

Statement	1	2	3	4
I feel a real compassion for other people. I can't stand by and see someone in distress.				
I find it easy to step in an pray for someone if they tell me they have a need.				
I am not afraid of getting my hands dirty. I am prepared to take a risk to do what God is asking me to do.				
I actively look for opportunities to demonstrate His strength through my faith.				

1 = Strongly Agree **2** = Agree **3** = Disagree **4** = Strongly Disagree

Leadership

Statement	**1**	**2**	**3**	**4**
I need to be involved in providing the solution. I don't have a lot of time for those who are just along for the ride.				
People tend to look to me for guidance, especially when they don't know what to do next.				
I like being the one to sort out a problem – especially if the answer is not immediately obvious.				
I prefer breaking new ground and find I need people around me who can fill in the details.				

Evangelism

Statement	**1**	**2**	**3**	**4**
I am always looking for opportunities to share my faith with others				
The fate of the unsaved concerns me greatly. I am passionate about seeing them saved – more than anything				
I regularly invite and bring people to church				
I have had a lot of success in seeing people won to Christ				

1 = Strongly Agree **2** = Agree **3** = Disagree **4** = Strongly Disagree

Teaching

Statement	1	2	3	4
When I read my Bible, I like to take notes on what I have learned from the passage I am reading.				
I also take notes in Church and review them later to think through the implications of what has been said.				
I love to read and listen to other people's interpretation of the Word. I find that I want to pass on what I have learned to other people.				
I find that people often ask me to explain things when they don't understand them.				
I like to read and study, and not just the Bible.				
I am happy to give my opinion and I find that people are generally receptive to my ideas.				

Administration/ Service

Statement	1	2	3	4
The vision thing is OK, but what I really want is a concrete plan of action. I need to know the details before I start.				
I am a realist – it is almost always a question of prioritisation. I am not easily distracted by the trivial.				
I like to think things through before I jump in. I believe in detailed planning before action.				
I am the person to go to when people are looking for a way to make things happen.				
I invariably end up being a part of a team, but rarely lead. If I am honest, I am more comfortable that way.				

1 = Strongly Agree **2** = Agree **3** = Disagree **4** = Strongly Disagree

Exhortation / Giving / Mercy

Statement	1	2	3	4
I enjoy giving hope to those in need				
I am very compassionate to those in need				
I have the desire to learn more about counselling so I can help others				
I enjoy seeing people respond to encouragement.				
I am confident that God will take care of my needs when I give sacrificially and cheerfully.				
I enjoy giving money to the needy.				
I would like to have a ministry for those who are needy.				

Homework

The Use of Spiritual Gifts

Read 1 Corinthians 12:12-27 and answer the following:

Discuss what happens when we make judgments about the attractiveness, or otherwise, of various gifts. What are some of the dangers of making such judgments?

How can we make sure we are placing value on the gifts that may appear less attractive to us?

How do I make sure that I have been placed in the body '...just as he desired' – 1 Corinthians 12: 18?

Putting it into Practice

Before the next class take note of a time where one of the spiritual gifts has been exercised in a service, gathering, team or small group you were involved in. Answer the following questions:

Which of the gifts was being exercised and what was the role of the person exercising it?

Is this gift exercised regularly in this context and, if so, does it tend to be the same person in the group who exercised it?

What was the net effect of the exercise of the gift? How did you/others feel about the gift being exercised in this context?

Week 5

Introduction

Session 1 – The Church and Leadership (Part 1)
Biblical Foundation

Break

Session 2 – The Church and Leadership (Part 2)
How Does God Raise and Develop Leaders?

Session 3 – Where Am I on My Leadership Journey?

Homework – The Leadership Development of Peter

Session 1

The Church and Leadership (Part 1)

Outcomes

By the end of this session, you will be able to:

* Prove and explain, from scripture, that leadership, especially local church leadership, is a biblical principle
* Explain, from scripture, why God uses leadership to govern the Church

The Biblical Foundation for Leadership

Session 2

The Church and Leadership (Part 2)

Outcomes

By the end of this session, you will be able to:

* Describe, from Scripture, the principles and processes involved in God's calling, developing and releasing of leaders
* Describe how these principles are/can be implemented in church life and their own life

How Does God Raise and Develop Leaders?

Session 3
Where Am I On My Leadership Journey?

Complete the following questionnaire to evaluate where you are as a leader, and identify some of the steps you can take to move forward.

Instructions

For each quality, give yourself a rating out of 5, where:

1 = Never
2 = Sometimes
3 = About half the time
4 = Most of the time
5 = Always

In the qualities that need work, write down some of the things you could do to grow.

Personal Leadership

Statement	Rating	Growth Ideas
I have a clear sense of God's plan for my life, and set and reach goals to fulfil it.		
I have a fresh and satisfying walk with God, where I hear His voice.		
I plan and manage my time, making the best use of it, getting the most important things done.		
I am satisfied with my relationships – I have great friendships and am making new ones.		
My financial affairs are in order; I budget my expenditure; I pay my bills on time; I give generously and wisely.		

Table continued on the next page...

I have experienced leaders I respect speaking into my life.		
I regularly and frequently attend and serve in my local church.		
I am learning new things through formal or informal study.		
I overcome problems with a positive, creative and determined approach.		
I have a positive, enthusiastic and optimistic attitude.		
I regularly exercising, eat well, and manage the stress in my life.		

Being in a Team (Church and Work)

Statement	Rating	Growth Ideas
I get on well with others in my team.		
I get on well with my leader.		
I do my job excellently.		
My leader relies on me and gives me extra responsibilities.		
I understand what my leader wants.		
I resolve conflicts well with other team members.		

Table continued on the next page...

I have taken my role on the team forward.		
I have helped other people on the team grow.		
My communication is clear, considerate and positive.		
I contribute to new and creative ideas and solutions to problems.		
I take responsibility.		
I follow through on what I am given to do.		

Leading Others

Statement	Rating	Growth Ideas
I attract and recruit people to my team.		
I understand the strengths and weaknesses of my team members.		
I assign responsibilities to people that they find meaningful and able to excel at.		
I make decisions readily.		
I develop others, so that their personal lives and their leadership move forward.		

Table continued on the next page...

I resolve conflicts in my team		
I plan, allocate and manage the work I give others		
I delegate responsibility to people easily		
I coach people in their roles so they can succeed		
I lead team meetings in a way that builds and strengthens the team		
The atmosphere in my team is positive, encouraging, fun		
I encourage people on my team		

Homework

The Leadership Development of Peter

Read the account in **Luke 5:1-11** of one of the early examples of Jesus' input into Peter, one of His key leaders and answer the following questions:

What lessons do you think Jesus was trying to teach Peter? What difference did it make in his life?

What did Peter learn about Jesus from this event? How did it affect his leadership?

Now read the account of Peter's denial of Jesus in **Mark 14:27-30** and Jesus' restoration of him in **John 21:15-19** and answer the following questions:

What do you think this event taught Peter about himself?

What do we learn about Jesus' leadership from this event?

How would Peter's leadership be different after this experience?

Now read the account in **Acts 3:1-26** and answer the following questions:
What changes or adjustments had Peter made by this stage of his life? Can you see evidence of his having learnt from his experience?

What things can you apply to your leadership journey from these three events in Peter's life?

Week 6

Introduction

Session 1 – The Church and Leadership (Part 3)
The Role of Leadership

Break

Session 2 – Me and My Church (Part 1)
Belonging

Session 3 – How Can I Contribute to the Health of the Church

Homework– The Perfect Model

Session 1

The Church and Leadership (Part 3)

Outcomes

By the end of this session, you will be able to:

* Explain the importance of health, unity and purpose to a local church or a ministry team
* Give biblical examples of leaders who used their leadership to achieve health, unity and purpose amongst their followers
* Explain how leaders go about using leadership and influence to build unity, health and purpose

The Role of Leadership

Session 2

Me and The Church (Part 1)

Outcomes

By the end of this session, you will be able to:

* Describe the benefits they (and others) receive from finding “belonging” in being part of the church
* Describe the actions they can take to find and experience “belonging” in church
* Describe the actions they can take to help others find and experience “belonging” in church

Belonging

Session 3

How Can I Contribute to the Health Of the Church?

Discuss the following questions in a small group setting.

* How do you feel when you "belong"?
* When a person is involved in a Connect Group (mid-week small group) or in serving in church in a ministry team, how does this enhance their sense of "belonging"?
* What personal hindrances might a person have that makes it difficult for them to connect and feel like they belong? What could be done to help them become more connected?
* In a large group (E.g., before or after church) what practical steps can you take to make sure that others feel part of the "in" crowd (E.g., part of the family)?
* What qualities make someone good at getting people connected and involved? Why do those qualities work?
* How could my development and actions as a leader help other people connect, get involved and belong?

Connecting somebody

Each of you identify one person in your world you can reach out to connect or involve so that they can feel like they belong:

* Brainstorm ideas of how you can go about that
* Pray for that person as a group and what you're about to do to connect them

Personal Evaluation Question – Your Sense of Belonging:

* How would you rate your sense of belonging in church?
* What can you do to take it to the next level?
* Are you prepared to let someone hold you accountable to do what you need to do? Why not take action this week.

Homework
The Perfect Model

Read Philippians 2:1-11 and Luke 10:29-37

Identify and list the similarities found in these scriptures in the context of what we have learnt over the past six weeks in this Leadership course.

What was Jesus' attitude to servanthood, as represented in Philippians?

From your reading of the Luke passage, build a profile of a servant leader. Explain why you have chosen those specific characteristics.

Week 7

Introduction

Session 1 – The Church and Leadership (Part 4)

Servant Leadership
Authority and Submission

Break

Session 2 – Me and My Church (Part 2)

Significance

Session 3 – How am I as a Servant Leader?

Session 1

The Church and Leadership (Part 4)

Outcomes

By the end of this session, you will be able to:

* Explain the biblical concept of "servant leadership" – what it does and does not mean
* Describe the ways that strong leadership is servant leadership, and the benefits that those being lead derive from it
* Explain the biblical principles of authority and submission, and describe how they apply to leading and following

Servant Leadership

Authority & Submission

Session 2

Me and The Church (Part 2)

Outcomes

By the end of this session, you will be able to:

* Describe people's need for significance and how involvement in church develops a sense of significance
* Describe some key ideas for how to (and how not to) develop significance through serving in church
* Explain why and how our significance is enhanced through being on team

Significance

Session 3
How am I as a Servant Leader?

In this exercise we will be exploring a leadership scenario that might arise in church, and using it to understand how servant leadership might operate. We'll also use it so that you can reflect on where you might be up to in your development as a servant leader. This exercise is performed in a small group.

Step 1 – Leadership Scenario

Imagine you are the leader of the New Christians team at church on the weekend.

There are a number of things that need to be done before, during and after a service.

For example:

★ Before the service, there is a team meeting before the service, Bibles and address cards need to be given to team members, some training is done and roles and positions during the service are allocated

★ During the service, new people are greeted, and people who make a decision for Christ are spoken to, to encourage them to go on with Christ and connect to church

★ After the service, new Christian classes are conducted, name and address information is gathered and entered in a database, and a debriefing is held

Step 2 – A Problem in the Team – The Impact

One of your team members has been coming late and leaving early on a regular basis over the last couple of months. When they are there they are disengaged and unhelpful.

As a group brainstorm the impact of this person's behaviour on the team, and on new people and new Christians in that service.

Question: What should the leader do about the situation and why?

Step 3 – Role Plays

Now, select two people to role play a conversation between 'the leader' and the 'team member'. (There are four different scenarios, so rotate amongst the group.)

Scene 1A
The Team Leader is task-focused, demanding and insensitive and the Team Member is experiencing some significant personal challenges in their family.

Debrief: What was wrong with this scenario? How would a servant leader handle this situation?

Scene 1B
The Team Leader is a servant leader and the Team Member is experiencing some significant personal challenges in their family.

Scene 2A
The Team Leader doesn't like confrontation, and wants people to like them, and the Team Member just has a bad attitude and doesn't care.

Debrief: What was wrong with this scenario? How would a servant-leader handle this situation?

Scene 2B
The Team Leader is a servant leader and Team Member just has a bad attitude and doesn't care.

Step 4 – Debrief

What do you learn about Servant Leadership from this exercise?
What qualities are required of servant leaders?